Easy Cc Cookbook

The Effortless Chef Series

By
Chef Maggie Chow
Copyright © 2015 by Saxonberg Associates
All rights reserved

Published by
BookSumo, a division of Saxonberg Associates
http://www.booksumo.com/

STAY TO THE END OF THE COOKBOOK AND RECEIVE....

I really appreciate when people, take the time to read all of my recipes.

So, as a gift for reading this entire cookbook you will receive a **massive collection of Sushi Recipes**.

The recipes in *Infinite Sushi: A Complete Set of Sushi Recipes* are the best and easiest.

Sushi can be quite expensive in stores, but when made at home it is quite easy.

You'll learn all the classics like: Sushi Rice, California Rolls, Smoked Salmon, and so much more!

So enjoy this cookbook and continue the adventure with some great Sushi!

About the Author.

Maggie Chow is the author and creator of your favorite *Easy Cookbooks* and *The Effortless Chef Series*. Maggie is a lover of all things related to food. Maggie loves nothing more than finding new recipes, trying them out, and then making them her own, by adding or removing ingredients, tweaking cooking times, and anything to make the recipe not only taste better, but be easier to cook!

For a complete listing of all my books please see my author page.

INTRODUCTION

Welcome to *The Effortless Chef Series*! Thank you for taking the time to download the *Easy Couscous Cookbook*. Come take a journey with me into the delights of easy cooking. The point of this cookbook and all my cookbooks is to exemplify the effortless nature of cooking simply.

In this book we focus on Couscous. You will find that even though the recipes are simple, the taste of the dishes is quite amazing.

So will you join me in an adventure of simple cooking? If the answer is yes (and I hope it is) please consult the table of contents to find the dishes you are most interested in. Once you are ready jump right in and start cooking.

— Chef Maggie Chow

Table of Contents

Stay To the End of the Cookbook and Receive....................................... 2
About the Author.................................. 4
Introduction 6
Table of Contents 7
Any Issues? Contact Me 15
Legal Notes... 16
Common Abbreviations...................... 17
Chapter 1: Easy Couscous Recipes...... 18
    Couscous I....................................... 18
    (Tagine) 18
    (Moroccan Style I) 18
    Couscous II 22
    (Savory, Almonds, and Tomatoes) .. 22
    Couscous III.................................... 25

(Sun Dried Tomatoes, Olives, Feta, and Garbanzos) 25

(Greek Style) 25

Couscous IV 28

(Quinoa, Onions, and Farro) 28

Couscous V 31

(Garlic, Corn, Black Beans, Lime, and Jalapenos) 31

(Mexican Style) 31

Couscous VI 34

(Almonds, Raisins, and Lemon) 34

(Moroccan Style II) 34

Couscous VII 37

(Jalapenos, Peas, and Mint) 37

Couscous VIII 40

(Chicken, Cucumbers, and Parsley) 40

Couscous IX 43

(Lime and Chicken) 43

Couscous X 46

(Peppers, Corn, and Black Beans) ... 46

Couscous XI 49

(Creamy Parsley, Chickpeas, and Almonds) 49
Couscous XII 52
(Veggie Turkey Couscous Bits) 52
Couscous XIII 55
(Squash and Garbanzos) 55
(Moroccan Style III) 55
Couscous XIV 58
(Cherry Tomatoes, Onions, and Basil) 58
Couscous XV 61
(Mangos, and Salsa) 61
Couscous XVI 64
(Moroccan Salmon Cake) 64
Couscous XVII 67
(Feta, Balsamic, and Asparagus) 67
Couscous XVIII 70
(Peppers, Cucumbers, and Olives) .. 70
(Greek Style II) 70
Couscous XIX 73

(Cloves, Onions, Tomatoes, and Chicken) 73
(Moroccan Style IV) 73
Couscous XX 77
(Almonds, Cilantro, and Curry) 77
Couscous XXI 80
(Spicy Chicken and Carrots) 80
Couscous XXII 83
(Peppers, Shrimp, and Feta) 83
Couscous XXIII 86
(Pepper, Lemon, and Cilantro) 86
Couscous XXIV 89
(Lemons, Parsley, Basil, Lettuce) 89
Couscous XXV 92
(Creamy Mushrooms and Pork) 92
Couscous XXVI 95
(Breakfast I) 95
Couscous XXVII 98
(Apricots, Raisins, Almonds, and Dates) 98
(Moroccan Style V) 98

Couscous XXVIII 101

(Garlic, Roma Tomatoes, and Monterey) 101

Couscous XXVIII 104

(Tomatoes, Mozzarella, Basil, and Mint) 104

Couscous XXX 107

(Almonds, Ham, Ginger, and Broccoli) 107

Couscous XXXI 110

(Feta, Cucumbers, Jalapenos, Basil, and Cilantro) 110

Couscous XXXII 113

(Peppers, Garlic, Onions, Mushrooms, and Dates) 113

Couscous XXXIII 116

(Cucumbers, Capers, and Dates) ... 116

Couscous XXXIV 119

(Kebabs) 119

(Moroccan Style VI 119

Couscous XXXV 123

(Carrots, Harissa, Peppers, Chicken, and Sausage) 123

Couscous XXXVI 127

(Garlic, Kale, and Parmesan) 127

Couscous XXXVII 130

(Savory, Parsley, Lemon, and Tomatoes) 130

Couscous XXXVIII 133

(Buttery Chives and Cheddar) 133

Couscous XXXIX 136

(Tomatoes and Tarragon) 136

Couscous XL 139

(Pine Nuts, Currants, and Pork) 139

Couscous XLI 142

(Bacon, Balsamic, and Curry) 142

Couscous XLII 145

(Pecans, Parmesan, and Pesto) 145

Couscous XLIII 148

(Honey Rutabaga) 148

Couscous XLIV 151

(Green Beans and Black Beans) 151

Couscous XLV	154
(Tabbouleh I)	154
Couscous XLVI	157
(Scallops, Parsley, and Parmesan)	157
Couscous XLVII	160
(Lentils, Onions, Feta, and Cranberries)	160
Couscous XLVIII	163
(Pine Nuts and Oranges)	163
Couscous XLIX	165
(Buttery Rosemary)	165
Couscous L	168
(Mexican Pineapple and Beans)	168
Couscous LI	171
(Crab, Clams, Bok Choy, and Tomatoes)	171
Couscous LII	174
(Saffron and Harissa)	174
(Persian Style)	174
THANKS FOR READING! NOW LET'S TRY SOME SUSHI....	177

Come On... 179
Let's Be Friends :)............................ 179
Can I Ask A Favour? 180
Interested in Other Easy Cookbooks?
.... 181

Any Issues? Contact Me

If you find that something important to you is missing from this book please contact me at maggie@booksumo.com.

I will try my best to re-publish a revised copy taking your feedback into consideration and let you know when the book has been revised with you in mind.

:)

— Chef Maggie Chow

Legal Notes

ALL RIGHTS RESERVED. NO PART OF THIS BOOK MAY BE REPRODUCED OR TRANSMITTED IN ANY FORM OR BY ANY MEANS. PHOTOCOPYING, POSTING ONLINE, AND / OR DIGITAL COPYING IS STRICTLY PROHIBITED UNLESS WRITTEN PERMISSION IS GRANTED BY THE BOOK'S PUBLISHING COMPANY. LIMITED USE OF THE BOOK'S TEXT IS PERMITTED FOR USE IN REVIEWS WRITTEN FOR THE PUBLIC AND/OR PUBLIC DOMAIN.

COMMON ABBREVIATIONS

cup(s)	C.
tablespoon	tbsp
teaspoon	tsp
ounce	oz.
pound	lb

*All units used are standard American measurements

Chapter 1: Easy Couscous Recipes

Couscous I

(Tagine)

(Moroccan Style I)

Ingredients

- 2 tbsps olive oil
- 8 skinless, boneless chicken thighs, cut into 1-inch pieces
- 1 eggplant, cut into 1 inch cubes
- 2 large onions, thinly sliced
- 4 large carrots, thinly sliced
- 1/2 C. dried cranberries
- 1/2 C. chopped dried apricots
- 2 C. chicken broth
- 2 tbsps tomato paste
- 2 tbsps lemon juice

- 2 tbsps all-purpose flour
- 2 tsps garlic salt
- 1 1/2 tsps ground cumin
- 1 1/2 tsps ground ginger
- 1 tsp cinnamon
- 3/4 tsp ground black pepper
- 1 C. water
- 1 C. couscous

Directions

- Get a bowl, mix until smooth: black pepper, broth, cinnamon, tomato paste, ginger, flour, cumin, and garlic salt.
- Stir fry your chicken in olive oil until browned all over but still slightly uncooked.
- Now put the chicken into your crock pot along with the eggplant. Then add: apricots, onions, cranberries, and carrots.
- Add the broth mix too.
- For 5 hrs cook with the high setting.

- Now get a big pot and get your water boiling.
- Once it is boiling pour in your couscous.
- Get the mix boiling again, then place a lid on the pot and shut the heat.
- Let the couscous sit in the hot water for 7 mins. Then stir it.
- When the chicken is finished serve over the couscous.
- Enjoy.

Amount per serving (8 total)

Timing Information:

Preparation	Cooking	Total Time
30 m	5 h	5 h 30 m

Nutritional Information:

Calories	380 kcal
Fat	15.2 g
Carbohydrates	38.5g
Protein	22.3 g
Cholesterol	65 mg
Sodium	571 mg

* Percent Daily Values are based on a 2,000 calorie diet.

Couscous II

(Savory, Almonds, and Tomatoes)

Ingredients

- 1 C. water
- 1 tsp dried savory
- 1 tsp dried parsley
- 1 pinch crushed red pepper flakes
- 1 tbsp chicken bouillon granules
- 1/2 C. pearl (Israeli) couscous
- 1 lemon, zest grated
- 1/2 C. toasted slivered almonds
- 1/2 C. chopped celery
- 1/3 C. chopped onion
- 1/2 tomato, seeded and chopped
- 1 tbsp olive oil
- salt and black pepper to taste

Directions

- Boil the following for 2 mins: bouillon, savory, pepper flakes, and parsley.
- Now add the couscous and let it gently boil with a lower level of heat for 12 mins.
- Place a lid on the pot and shut the heat.
- Once the couscous has lost its heat remove any liquid that is left.
- Get a bowl, combine: olive oil, zest, tomato, almonds, couscous mix, onions, and celery.
- Add your preferred amount of pepper and salt and the place the contents in the fridge for at least 30 mins covered with plastic wrap.
- Enjoy.

Amount per serving (3 total)

Timing Information:

Preparation	Cooking	Total Time
20 m	10 m	1 h 30 m

Nutritional Information:

Calories	266 kcal
Fat	14.3 g
Carbohydrates	27g
Protein	7.9 g
Cholesterol	< 1 mg
Sodium	401 mg

* Percent Daily Values are based on a 2,000 calorie diet.

Couscous III

(Sun Dried Tomatoes, Olives, Feta, and Garbanzos)

(Greek Style)

Ingredients

- 1/4 C. chicken broth
- 1/2 C. water
- 1 tsp minced garlic
- 1/2 C. pearl (Israeli) couscous
- 1/4 C. chopped sun-dried tomatoes
- 1/4 C. sliced Kalamata olives
- 2 tbsps crumbled feta cheese
- 1 C. canned garbanzo beans, rinsed and drained
- 1 tsp dried oregano
- 1/2 tsp ground black pepper
- 1 tbsp white wine vinegar
- 1 1/2 tsps lemon juice

Directions

- Boil your garlic in the broth for 3 mins. Then add in your couscous.
- Place a lid on the pot and shut the heat.
- Let the couscous sit in the hot water for 7 mins and then stir it.
- Get a bowl, combine: black pepper, beans, vinegar, tomatoes, oregano, lemon juice, cheese, olives, and couscous.
- Stir the mix and serve at room temp.
- Enjoy.

Amount per serving (3 total)

Timing Information:

Preparation	Cooking	Total Time
20 m	5 m	45 m

Nutritional Information:

Calories	254 kcal
Fat	5.6 g
Carbohydrates	42.4g
Protein	9 g
Cholesterol	6 mg
Sodium	592 mg

* Percent Daily Values are based on a 2,000 calorie diet.

Couscous IV

(Quinoa, Onions, and Farro)

Ingredients

- 6 1/2 C. water, divided
- 1 C. red quinoa
- 1 C. pearl (Israeli) couscous
- 1 C. farro
- 1 cucumber, seeded and chopped
- 1/2 red onion, chopped
- 1 orange bell pepper, seeded and chopped
- 1 yellow squash, seeded and chopped
- 1/2 C. extra-virgin olive oil
- 1 lemon, juiced
- 1/2 tsp kosher salt
- 1 (6 oz.) container crumbled feta cheese

Directions

- For 2 mins boil your quinoa in 2 C. of water. Then place a lid on the pot, set the heat to low, and the let quinoa cook for 17 mins.
- Simultaneously cook the couscous in boiling water (1.5 C.) for 12 mins in a covered pot.
- At the same time boil your farro for 26 mins in 3 C. of water, in a covered pot as well.
- Once everything is done get a bowl, combine: squash, quinoa, bell peppers, couscous, onions, cucumber and farro.
- Top with a dressing of: salt, lemon juice, and olive oil.
- Place a plastic covering over the bowl and cool it in the fridge for 1 hr.
- Before serving top the salad with some feta.
- Enjoy.

Amount per serving (8 total)

Timing Information:

Preparation	Cooking	Total Time
20 m	30 m	2 h 50 m

Nutritional Information:

Calories	424 kcal
Fat	20.9 g
Carbohydrates	50.3g
Protein	11.6 g
Cholesterol	19 mg
Sodium	370 mg

* Percent Daily Values are based on a 2,000 calorie diet.

Couscous V

(Garlic, Corn, Black Beans, Lime, and Jalapenos)

(Mexican Style)

Ingredients:

- 1 cup couscous
- 1/2 tsp ground cumin
- 1 tsp salt, or to taste
- 1 1/4 cups boiling water
- 1 clove unpeeled garlic
- 1 (15 oz.) can black beans, rinsed and drained
- 1 cup canned whole kernel corn, drained
- 1/2 cup finely chopped red onion
- 1/4 cup chopped fresh cilantro
- 1 jalapeno pepper, minced
- 3 tbsps olive oil
- 3 tbsps fresh lime juice, or to taste

Directions:

- Add boiling water into a mixture of salt and couscous in a large sized bowl, and cover it with plastic wrap before letting it stand for about ten minutes.
- In this time, cook unpeeled garlic in hot oil over medium heat until it has turned golden brown.
- Now mash this garlic and add it into the couscous along with black beans, onion, cilantro, corn, jalapeno pepper, olive oil, and lime juice.
- Serve.

Amount per serving (15 total)

Timing Information:

Preparation	Cooking	Total Time
15 min		25 min

Nutritional Information:

Calories	300 kcal
Carbohydrates	44.8 g
Cholesterol	0 mg
Fat	10.9 g
Fiber	3.6 g
Protein	7.1 g
Sodium	713 mg

* Percent Daily Values are based on a 2,000 calorie diet.

Couscous VI

(Almonds, Raisins, and Lemon)

(Moroccan Style II)

Ingredients

- 2 C. water
- 1 C. pearl (Israeli) couscous
- 1 tbsp olive oil
- 1/2 C. chopped yellow onion
- 1 shallot, chopped
- 6 cloves garlic, quartered
- 1/2 C. golden raisins
- 1/2 C. chopped oil-packed sun-dried tomatoes
- 1/2 C. slivered almonds
- 1/2 tsp kosher salt
- 1/4 tsp ground black pepper
- 3 tbsps lemon juice
- 1 tbsp butter, softened

Directions

- Boil your couscous, uncovered for 14 mins in water.
- Simultaneously stir fry your garlic, shallots, and onions for 17 mins in olive oil.
- Now add: almonds, raisins, and tomatoes.
- Cook for 7 more mins.
- Pour the couscous into the shallot mix and cook for 3 mins.
- Add some: lemon juice, pepper, and salt.
- Shut the heat and add in your butter, let it melt, before serving.
- Enjoy.

Amount per serving (6 total)

Timing Information:

Preparation	Cooking	Total Time
10 m	35 m	45 m

Nutritional Information:

Calories	265 kcal
Fat	10.3 g
Carbohydrates	38.6g
Protein	6.6 g
Cholesterol	5 mg
Sodium	208 mg

* Percent Daily Values are based on a 2,000 calorie diet.

Couscous VII

(Jalapenos, Peas, and Mint)

Ingredients

- 2 C. dry couscous
- 1/2 C. chopped green onions
- 1 fresh jalapeno pepper, finely diced
- 2 tbsps olive oil
- 1/2 tsp ground cumin
- 1 pinch cayenne pepper
- 1 pinch ground black pepper
- 2 C. vegetable stock
- 1 bunch asparagus, trimmed and cut into 1/4-inch pieces
- 1 C. shelled fresh or thawed frozen peas
- 2 tbsps chopped fresh mint
- salt and freshly ground black pepper to taste

Directions

- Get a bowl, mix: black pepper, couscous, cayenne, onions, cumin, olive oil, and jalapenos.
- Get your peas and asparagus boiling in the veggie stock and then pour it into the bowl.
- Stir the couscous into the liquid and place a covering on the bowl.
- Let the mix sit for 12 mins then stir it.
- Add some mint, pepper, and salt before serving.
- Enjoy.

Amount per serving (6 total)

Timing Information:

Preparation	Cooking	Total Time
15 m	20 m	35 m

Nutritional Information:

Calories	306 kcal
Fat	5.3 g
Carbohydrates	53.7g
Protein	10.9 g
Cholesterol	0 mg
Sodium	228 mg

* Percent Daily Values are based on a 2,000 calorie diet.

Couscous VIII

(Chicken, Cucumbers, and Parsley)

Ingredients

- 2 C. chicken broth
- 1 (10 oz.) box couscous
- 3/4 C. olive oil
- 1/4 C. fresh lemon juice
- 2 tbsps white balsamic vinegar
- 1/4 C. chopped fresh rosemary leaves
- salt and ground black pepper to taste
- 2 large cooked skinless, boneless chicken breast halves, cut into bite-size pieces
- 1 C. chopped English cucumber
- 1/2 C. chopped sun-dried tomatoes
- 1/2 C. chopped pitted kalamata olives
- 1/2 C. crumbled feta cheese

- 1/3 C. chopped fresh Italian parsley
- salt and ground black pepper to taste

Directions

- Get your stock boiling then add in your couscous.
- Place a lid on the pot and shut the heat.
- Let the contents sit for 7 mins before stirring.
- Blend: vinegar, olive oil, and lemon juice with some rosemary.
- Now add some pepper and salt before continuing.
- Get a bowl, mix: tomatoes, parsley, couscous, feta, cucumbers, and chicken.
- Cover the couscous with the dressing and add a bit more if you like also add some more pepper and salt too.
- Enjoy.

Amount per serving (6 total)

Timing Information:

Preparation	Cooking	Total Time
35 m	10 m	45 m

Nutritional Information:

Calories	645 kcal
Fat	38.8 g
Carbohydrates	44g
Protein	29.4 g
Cholesterol	68 mg
Sodium	792 mg

* Percent Daily Values are based on a 2,000 calorie diet.

Couscous IX

(Lime and Chicken)

Ingredients

- 1 tbsp olive oil
- 1 lb skinless, boneless chicken breast halves, cubed
- 1 pinch monosodium glutamate (MSG)
- 6 tbsps soy sauce
- 6 tbsps brown sugar
- 1/2 tsp red pepper flakes, or more to taste
- 1 lime, juiced and zested
- 2 C. vegetable broth
- 1 C. couscous
- 1/3 C. chopped cilantro
- 4 wedges lime for garnish

Directions

- Get a bowl, combine: zest, soy sauce, lime juice, sugar, and pepper flakes.
- Boil everything gently for 4 mins until it becomes sauce like.
- Now stir fry your chicken until it is fully done in olive oil for 7 mins.
- Add in your MSG while it fries.
- Then top everything with the lime sauce and continue stir frying for 4 more mins.
- Let your couscous sit in the veggie broth that was boiling for 7 mins in a covered pot.
- Place some couscous on a plate for serving and add a topping of lime chicken.
- Garnish with freshly squeezed lime from the wedges.
- Enjoy.

Amount per serving (4 total)

Timing Information:

Preparation	Cooking	Total Time
15 m	15 m	35 m

Nutritional Information:

Calories	380 kcal
Fat	6.2 g
Carbohydrates	52g
Protein	28.4 g
Cholesterol	59 mg
Sodium	1675 mg

* Percent Daily Values are based on a 2,000 calorie diet.

Couscous X

(Peppers, Corn, and Black Beans)

Ingredients

- 1 C. uncooked couscous
- 1 1/4 C. chicken broth
- 3 tbsps extra virgin olive oil
- 2 tbsps fresh lime juice
- 1 tsp red wine vinegar
- 1/2 tsp ground cumin
- 8 green onions, chopped
- 1 red bell pepper, seeded and chopped
- 1/4 C. chopped fresh cilantro
- 1 C. frozen corn kernels, thawed
- 2 (15 oz.) cans black beans, drained
- salt and pepper to taste

Directions

- Get your broth boiling for 2 mins then add in your couscous.
- Place a lid on the pot and shut the heat.
- Let the couscous sit in the hot water for 7 mins, before stirring it.
- Get a bowl, mix: beans, olive oil, couscous, corn, lime juice, cilantro, vinegar, red pepper, onions, and cumin.
- Add your preferred amount of pepper and salt. Then place a plastic covering around the bowl, let the mix sit in the fridge for 20 to 30 mins before serving.
- Enjoy.

Amount per serving (8 total)

Timing Information:

Preparation	Cooking	Total Time
30 m		35 m

Nutritional Information:

Calories	255 kcal
Fat	5.9 g
Carbohydrates	41.2g
Protein	10.4 g
Cholesterol	< 1 mg
Sodium	565 mg

* Percent Daily Values are based on a 2,000 calorie diet.

Couscous XI

(Creamy Parsley, Chickpeas, and Almonds)

Ingredients

- 1/2 C. creamy salad dressing
- 1/4 C. plain yogurt
- 1 tsp ground cumin
- salt and pepper to taste
- 1 tbsp butter
- 1/2 C. couscous
- 1 C. water
- 1 red onion, chopped
- 1 red bell pepper, chopped
- 1/3 C. chopped parsley
- 1/3 C. raisins
- 1/3 C. toasted and sliced almonds
- 1/2 C. canned chickpeas, drained

Directions

- Get a bowl, combine: pepper, salad dressing, salt, cumin, and yogurt.
- Cover the bowl with some plastic wrap and chill in the fridge for 1 h.
- Simultaneously toast your couscous in butter for 2 mins then add your water.
- Get everything boiling, then place a lid on the pot, set the heat to low and let the contents gently boil for 7 mins.
- Get your dressing mix and add in: chickpeas, couscous, almonds, red onions, raisins, parsley, and bell peppers.
- Place the covering back on the bowl and put it back in the fridge for 20 mins.
- Enjoy.

Amount per serving (6 total)

Timing Information:

Preparation	Cooking	Total Time
15 m	30 m	1 h 45 m

Nutritional Information:

Calories	247 kcal
Fat	12.2 g
Carbohydrates	30g
Protein	5.7 g
Cholesterol	13 mg
Sodium	251 mg

* Percent Daily Values are based on a 2,000 calorie diet.

Couscous XII

(Veggie Turkey Couscous Bits)

Ingredients

- 2 C. coarsely chopped zucchini
- 1 1/2 C. coarsely chopped onions
- 1 red bell pepper, coarsely chopped
- 1 lb extra lean ground turkey
- 1/2 C. uncooked couscous
- 1 egg
- 2 tbsps Worcestershire sauce
- 1 tbsp Dijon mustard
- 1/2 C. barbecue sauce, or as needed

Directions

- Coat your muffin pan with non-stick spray and then set your oven

to 400 degrees before doing anything else.
- Blend with a few pulses: bell peppers, zucchini, and onions. Then add them to a bowl, with: mustard, turkey, Worcestershire, eggs, and couscous.
- Evenly divide the mix between the sections in your muffin pan then add bbq sauce to each (1 tsp).
- Cook everything in the oven for 27 mins.
- Check the temperature of each, it should be 160 degrees.
- Let the dish sit for 10 mins before serving.
- Enjoy.

Amount per serving (10 total)

Timing Information:

Preparation	Cooking	Total Time
20 m	25 m	50 m

Nutritional Information:

Calories	119 kcal
Fat	1 g
Carbohydrates	13.6g
Protein	13.2 g
Cholesterol	47 mg
Sodium	244 mg

* Percent Daily Values are based on a 2,000 calorie diet.

Couscous XIII

(Squash and Garbanzos)

(Moroccan Style III)

Ingredients

- 2 tbsps brown sugar
- 1 tbsp butter, melted
- 2 large acorn squash, halved and seeded
- 2 tbsps olive oil
- 2 cloves garlic, chopped
- 2 stalks celery, chopped
- 2 carrots, chopped
- 1 C. garbanzo beans, drained
- 1/2 C. raisins
- 1 1/2 tbsps ground cumin
- salt and pepper to taste
- 1 (14 oz.) can chicken broth
- 1 C. uncooked couscous

Directions

- Set your oven to 350 degrees before doing anything else.
- Cook your squash for 32 mins in the oven. Then top the squash with a mix of butter and sugar that has been melted and stirred together.
- Stir fry, for 7 mins, in olive oil: carrots, celery, and garlic.
- Now add the raisins and beans.
- Fry the contents until everything is soft then add in pepper, salt, and cumin.
- Add the broth to the carrot mix and then add the couscous.
- Place a lid on the pot and place the pot to the side away from all heat.
- Let the contents sit for 7 mins.
- Fill your squashes with the couscous mix.
- Enjoy.

Amount per serving (4 total)

Timing Information:

Preparation	Cooking	Total Time
15 m	45 m	1 h

Nutritional Information:

Calories	502 kcal
Fat	11.7 g
Carbohydrates	93.8g
Protein	11.2 g
Cholesterol	10 mg
Sodium	728 mg

* Percent Daily Values are based on a 2,000 calorie diet.

Couscous XIV

(Cherry Tomatoes, Onions, and Basil)

Ingredients

- 1 C. couscous
- 1 C. boiling water
- 3 tbsps olive oil
- 1 clove garlic, minced
- 1/4 C. diced red bell pepper
- 4 green onions, sliced
- 1 C. cherry tomatoes
- 1 C. fresh basil leaves
- 1 pinch salt
- 1 pinch ground black pepper
- 1 dash balsamic vinegar
- 1/4 C. grated Parmesan cheese

Directions

- Set your oven to 350 degrees before doing anything else.

- Get your water boiling then pour in your couscous.
- Get everything boiling again. Then place a lid on the pot, shut the heat, and let the mix sit for 7 mins before stirring.
- Simultaneously stir fry your peppers, onions, and garlic for 3 mins then add: pepper, tomatoes, salt, basil, and couscous.
- Pour everything into a baking dish and add in your balsamic.
- Cook everything in the oven for 25 mins then add the parmesan.
- Enjoy.

Amount per serving (4 total)

Timing Information:

Preparation	Cooking	Total Time
5 m	35 m	40 m

Nutritional Information:

Calories	299 kcal
Fat	12.4 g
Carbohydrates	38g
Protein	9.1 g
Cholesterol	6 mg
Sodium	196 mg

* Percent Daily Values are based on a 2,000 calorie diet.

Couscous XV

(Mangos, and Salsa)

Ingredients

- 1 1/2 C. water
- 1 C. couscous
- 2/3 C. dried mango, diced
- 3/4 C. prepared salsa
- 2 tsps ground cumin
- 1 tsp curry powder

Directions

- Get the following boiling in a big pot: curry, couscous, water, cumin, mango, and salsa.
- Place a lid on the pot and set the heat to low.
- Cook everything for 4 mins and then let the contents sit for 7 more mins. Stir the couscous before plating.

- Enjoy.

Amount per serving (4 total)

Timing Information:

Preparation	Cooking	Total Time
10 m	5 m	20 m

Nutritional Information:

Calories	186 kcal
Fat	0.9 g
Carbohydrates	40.2g
Protein	5.1 g
Cholesterol	0 mg
Sodium	314 mg

* Percent Daily Values are based on a 2,000 calorie diet.

Couscous XVI

(Moroccan Salmon Cake)

Ingredients

Mayo Topping:

- 1/2 C. mayonnaise
- 1 clove garlic, crushed
- 1/8 tsp paprika

Salmon Cake:

- 1/2 C. couscous
- 2/3 C. orange juice
- 1 (14.75 oz.) can red salmon, drained
- 1 (10 oz.) package frozen chopped spinach, thawed, drained and squeezed dry
- 2 egg yolks, beaten
- 2 cloves garlic, crushed
- 1 tsp ground cumin

- 1/2 tsp ground black pepper
- 1/2 tsp salt
- 3 tbsps olive oil

Directions

- Get a bowl, mix: paprika, mayo, and garlic.
- Boil your orange juice in a large pot, then add in your couscous.
- Get the mix boiling again and then place a lid on the pot, shut the heat, and let the couscous stand for 7 mins.
- Now stir your couscous after it has lost all of its heat.
- Get a 2nd bowl, combine: salt, salmon, black pepper, spinach, cumin, egg yolks, and garlic.
- Shape this mix into patties and then fry them in olive oil for 8 mins turning each at 4 mins.
- When serving add a topping of mayo.
- Enjoy.

Amount per serving (4 total)

Timing Information:

Preparation	Cooking	Total Time
20 m	25 m	45 m

Nutritional Information:

Calories	620 kcal
Fat	46.4 g
Carbohydrates	26.4g
Protein	28.8 g
Cholesterol	178 mg
Sodium	950 mg

* Percent Daily Values are based on a 2,000 calorie diet.

Couscous XVII

(Feta, Balsamic, and Asparagus)

Ingredients

- 2 C. couscous
- 1 bunch fresh asparagus, trimmed and cut into 2-inch pieces
- 8 oz. grape tomatoes, halved
- 6 oz. feta cheese, crumbled
- 3 tbsps balsamic vinegar
- 2 tbsps extra-virgin olive oil
- Black pepper, to taste

Directions

- Boil your couscous in water, then place a lid on the pot, shut the heat, and let the couscous sit for 7 mins.
- Once it has cooled stir it with a fork.

- Simultaneously steam your asparagus over 2 inches of boiling water with a steamer insert and a pot. Steam the spears for 7 mins. Now remove all the liquid.
- Get a bowl, toss: couscous, olive oil, asparagus, balsamic, cheese, pepper, and tomatoes.
- Enjoy chilled or warm.

Amount per serving (4 total)

Timing Information:

Preparation	Cooking	Total Time
10 m	20 m	30 m

Nutritional Information:

Calories	541 kcal
Fat	16.7 g
Carbohydrates	77.7g
Protein	20.1 g
Cholesterol	38 mg
Sodium	494 mg

* Percent Daily Values are based on a 2,000 calorie diet.

Couscous XVIII

(Peppers, Cucumbers, and Olives)

(Greek Style II)

Ingredients

- 3 (6 oz.) packages garlic and herb couscous mix
- 1 pint cherry tomatoes, cut in half
- 1 (5 oz.) jar pitted kalamata olives, halved
- 1 C. mixed bell peppers (green, red, yellow, orange), diced
- 1 cucumber, sliced and then halved
- 1/2 C. parsley, finely chopped
- 1 (8 oz.) package crumbled feta cheese
- 1/2 C. Greek vinaigrette salad dressing

Directions

- Get your couscous boiling in water for 2 mins. Then place a lid on the pot, shut and heat, and it sit for 7 mins before stirring after it has cooled.
- Place the couscous in a bowl, and combine in: cheese, tomatoes, parsley, olives, cucumber, and bell peppers.
- Add in your Greek dressing and toss everything to coat evenly.
- Feel free to add more dressing if you like.
- Enjoy.

Amount per serving (20 total)

Timing Information:

Preparation	Cooking	Total Time
30 m	15 m	45 m

Nutritional Information:

Calories	159 kcal
Fat	6.5 g
Carbohydrates	21.4g
Protein	5.7 g
Cholesterol	10 mg
Sodium	642 mg

* Percent Daily Values are based on a 2,000 calorie diet.

Couscous XIX

(Cloves, Onions, Tomatoes, and Chicken)

(Moroccan Style IV)

Ingredients

- 1 C. whole wheat couscous
- 1 tbsp vegetable oil
- 1 medium onion, chopped
- 2 bay leaves
- 5 whole cloves, crushed
- 1/2 tsp cinnamon
- 1 tsp ground dried turmeric
- 1/4 tsp ground cayenne pepper
- 6 skinless, boneless chicken breast halves - chopped
- 1 (16 oz.) can garbanzo beans
- 1 (16 oz.) can crushed tomatoes
- 1 (48 fluid oz.) can chicken broth
- 2 carrots, cut into 1/2 inch pieces

- 1 zucchini, cut into 1/2-inch pieces
- salt to taste

Directions

- Get your couscous boiling in water for 2 mins. Then place a lid on the pot, shut and heat, and it sit for 7 mins before stirring once it has cooled.
- Stir fry your onions in oil until soft then add in: cayenne, bay leaves, turmeric, cloves, and cinnamon.
- Cook everything for 1 more min then pour in your chicken and cook it until browned all over.
- Once everything has been browned add in: broth, tomatoes, and beans.
- Get everything boiling.
- Lower the heat to low and gently boil for 27 mins.
- Now add your zucchini and carrots and also some salt.

- Continue for 12 more mins.
- Serve the veggies and chicken over the couscous.
- Enjoy.

Amount per serving (6 total)

Timing Information:

Preparation	Cooking	Total Time
15 m	45 m	1 h

Nutritional Information:

Calories	399 kcal
Fat	6.7 g
Carbohydrates	50.7g
Protein	33.4 g
Cholesterol	67 mg
Sodium	1539 mg

* Percent Daily Values are based on a 2,000 calorie diet.

Couscous XX

(Almonds, Cilantro, and Curry)

Ingredients

- 1 1/2 C. couscous
- 3 C. chicken stock
- 1 tbsp curry powder
- 2 tsps salt
- 1 tsp ground black pepper
- 2 tbsps extra-virgin olive oil
- 1/2 C. raisins
- 1 bunch cilantro, chopped
- 1/2 C. slivered almonds, toasted

Directions

- Boil the following then pour it over your couscous in a salad bowl: raisins, stock, olive oil, curry powder, pepper, and salt.

- Place some plastic wrap around the bowl, and let the couscous stand for 12 mins before stirring it.
- Serve the couscous with some almonds and cilantro.
- Enjoy.

Amount per serving (6 total)

Timing Information:

Preparation	Cooking	Total Time
10 m	10 m	30 m

Nutritional Information:

Calories	269 kcal
Fat	9.8 g
Carbohydrates	39.4g
Protein	7.1 g
Cholesterol	< 1 mg
Sodium	1131 mg

* Percent Daily Values are based on a 2,000 calorie diet.

Couscous XXI

(Spicy Chicken and Carrots)

Ingredients

- 3 1/4 C. low-sodium chicken broth
- 1 C. quick-cooking couscous
- 2 tbsps olive oil
- 4 skinless, boneless chicken breast halves - cut into cubes
- 1 pinch ground black pepper
- 1/2 C. finely chopped jalapeno chili peppers
- 1 carrot, thinly sliced
- 1 zucchini, diced
- 3 green onions, thinly sliced
- 1 1/2 tsps grated fresh ginger root
- 1 1/2 tsps curry powder
- 1/2 tsp ground coriander seed
- 1 tsp cornstarch

Directions

- Boil your broth (2 C.) and then add the couscous and olive oil. Place a lid on the pot and let the contents sit for 12 mins.
- Get a bowl, mix: cornstarch, 1 C. of broth, and curry.
- Coat your chicken with pepper then stir fry it in 1 tbsp of olive oil until fully done.
- Remove the chicken from the pan.
- Add in more olive oil and stir fry carrots and jalapenos for 4 mins then add: a quarter of a C. of broth, zucchini, ginger, and onions.
- Cook everything for 7 more mins.
- Add your cornstarch mix and cook for 3 more mins.
- Serve the spicy chicken and carrots over the couscous.
- Enjoy.

Amount per serving (4 total)

Timing Information:

Preparation	Cooking	Total Time
20 m	25 m	45 m

Nutritional Information:

Calories	415 kcal
Fat	11.5 g
Carbohydrates	40.6g
Protein	35.8 g
Cholesterol	75 mg
Sodium	177 mg

* Percent Daily Values are based on a 2,000 calorie diet.

Couscous XXII

(Peppers, Shrimp, and Feta)

Ingredients

- 2 C. couscous
- 2 C. water
- 3/4 C. olive oil
- 1/4 C. apple cider vinegar
- 1 tsp Dijon mustard
- 1 tsp ground cumin
- 1 clove garlic, crushed
- salt and pepper to taste
- 1 red bell pepper, chopped
- 1 yellow bell pepper, chopped
- 1 1/2 lbs cooked shrimp, peeled and deveined
- 2 medium tomatoes, chopped
- 1 C. chopped fresh parsley
- 1 C. crumbled feta cheese

Directions

- Boil your water then pour in your couscous, place a lid on the pot, and then let it sit for 7 mins and finally stir it once cooled.
- Get a bowl, combine: pepper, olive oil, salt, garlic, vinegar, and mustard.
- Get a bigger bowl, mix: cheese, shrimp, parsley, couscous, tomatoes, and bell peppers.
- Now combine in the vinegar mix and toss everything to coat.
- Place the mix in the fridge for 1 hr then serve.
- Enjoy.

Amount per serving (8 total)

Timing Information:

Preparation	Cooking	Total Time
30 m	5 m	35 m

Nutritional Information:

Calories	530 kcal
Fat	28.4 g
Carbohydrates	38.7g
Protein	28.7 g
Cholesterol	194 mg
Sodium	570 mg

* Percent Daily Values are based on a 2,000 calorie diet.

Couscous XXIII

(Pepper, Lemon, and Cilantro)

Ingredients

- 2 tbsps butter
- 2 tbsps olive oil
- 4 (4 oz.) salmon steaks
- 1 tsp minced garlic
- 1 tbsp lemon pepper
- 1 tsp salt
- 1/4 C. water
- 1 C. chopped fresh tomatoes
- 1 C. chopped fresh cilantro
- 2 C. boiling water
- 1 C. uncooked couscous

Directions

- Coat your salmon with salt, lemon pepper, and garlic.

- Now begin cooking it in olive oil and butter.
- Then add a quarter of a C. of water, cilantro, and tomatoes. Place a lid on the pan and cook for 16 mins.
- Simultaneously boil 2 C. of water then add in the couscous. Place a lid on the pot and the couscous stand for 7 mins.
- Top your salmon and couscous with any sauce in the pan when serving.
- Enjoy.

Amount per serving (4 total)

Timing Information:

Preparation	Cooking	Total Time
10 m	20 m	30 m

Nutritional Information:

Calories	498 kcal
Fat	23.5 g
Carbohydrates	36.2g
Protein	31.6 g
Cholesterol	89 mg
Sodium	1039 mg

* Percent Daily Values are based on a 2,000 calorie diet.

Couscous XXIV

(Lemons, Parsley, Basil, Lettuce)

Ingredients

- 10 oz. uncooked couscous
- 2 tbsps olive oil
- 1/2 C. lemon juice
- 3/4 tsp salt
- 1/4 tsp ground black pepper
- 1 cucumber, seeded and chopped
- 1/2 C. finely chopped green onions
- 1/2 C. fresh parsley, chopped
- 1/4 C. fresh basil, chopped
- 6 leaves lettuce
- 6 slices lemon

Directions

- Boil 1 and 3/4 C. of water then pour in the couscous.

- Let it boil for 2 mins before placing a lid on the pan and setting it to the side for 7 mins.
- Stir the contents after it has cooled off a bit.
- Get a bowl, mix: pepper, oil, salt, cucumber, couscous, onions, basil, parsley, and lemon juice.
- Serve the couscous over leaves of fresh lettuce and add some lemon as a topping on each plate.
- Enjoy.

Amount per serving (8 total)

Timing Information:

Preparation	Cooking	Total Time
10 m	10 m	1 h 20 m

Nutritional Information:

Calories	142 kcal
Fat	3.6 g
Carbohydrates	24.6g
Protein	4 g
Cholesterol	0 mg
Sodium	227 mg

* Percent Daily Values are based on a 2,000 calorie diet.

Couscous XXV

(Creamy Mushrooms and Pork)

Ingredients

- 1 tbsp vegetable oil
- 4 boneless pork chops, 3/4-inch thick
- 1 clove garlic, minced
- 1 (10.75 oz.) can Cream of Mushroom Soup
- 1/2 C. milk
- 4 C. hot cooked couscous or regular long-grain white rice

Directions

- Stir fry your pork for 12 mins in oil and then remove it from the pan.
- Add in your milk and soup and heat it until everything is boiling.

- Once it is boiling put the pork back in the pan and lower your heat to a simmer.
- Cook everything covered for 12 mins or until the pork is completely done.
- Enjoy over the couscous.

Amount per serving (4 total)

Timing Information:

Preparation	Cooking	Total Time
25 m		25 m

Nutritional Information:

Calories	376 kcal
Fat	11.1 g
Carbohydrates	40.1g
Protein	27.4 g
Cholesterol	66 mg
Sodium	463 mg

* Percent Daily Values are based on a 2,000 calorie diet.

Couscous XXVI

(Breakfast I)

Ingredients

- 2 C. skim milk
- 2 tbsps honey
- 3 tsps ground cinnamon
- 2 C. dry couscous
- 1/3 C. chopped dried apricots
- 1/3 C. raisins
- 1/2 C. slivered almonds

Directions

- Get the following boiling: cinnamon, honey, and milk.
- Add in the couscous and place a lid on the pot.
- Place the contents to the side away from the heat and let it sit for 7 mins.

- Now add your almonds, raisins, and apricots before serving.
- Enjoy.

Amount per serving (8 total)

Timing Information:

Preparation	Cooking	Total Time
5 m	5 m	10 m

Nutritional Information:

Calories	286 kcal
Fat	4.9 g
Carbohydrates	52.1g
Protein	9.9 g
Cholesterol	1 mg
Sodium	32 mg

* Percent Daily Values are based on a 2,000 calorie diet.

Couscous XXVII

(Apricots, Raisins, Almonds, and Dates)

(Moroccan Style V)

Ingredients

- 2 C. vegetable broth
- 5 tbsps unsalted butter
- 1/3 C. chopped dates
- 1/3 C. chopped dried apricots
- 1/3 C. golden raisins
- 2 C. dry couscous
- 3 tsps ground cinnamon
- 1/2 C. slivered almonds, toasted

Directions

- Get your broth boiling and then add in: raisins, butter, dates, and apricots.

- Continue the gentle boil for 4 more mins.
- Then add the couscous and a lid to the pot.
- Place everything to the side for 7 mins.
- Add your almonds that have been toasted for a few mins and your cinnamon.
- Stir the mix and then plate.
- Enjoy.

Amount per serving (6 total)

Timing Information:

Preparation	Cooking	Total Time
15 m	5 m	20 m

Nutritional Information:

Calories	442 kcal
Fat	14.8 g
Carbohydrates	68.2g
Protein	10.5 g
Cholesterol	25 mg
Sodium	164 mg

* Percent Daily Values are based on a 2,000 calorie diet.

Couscous XXVIII

(Garlic, Roma Tomatoes, and Monterey)

Ingredients

- 1 (10 oz.) box couscous
- 1 1/2 C. boiling water
- 2 tbsps olive oil
- 1/2 onion, diced
- 2 cloves garlic, minced
- 3 Roma (plum) tomatoes, diced
- 1/2 C. shredded Cheddar-Monterey Jack cheese blend

Directions

- Get a pot and boil your water in it. Pour it over your couscous in a bowl, and place a covering over everything.
- Let the contents sit for 12 mins.

- Once the couscous has cooled stir it.
- At the same time stir fry your garlic and onions for 7 mins then add in the tomatoes and cook until the juice of the tomatoes begins to become thick.
- Add in the couscous as well as the cheese, and cook for 2 more mins or until the cheese has melted.
- Plate and serve.
- Enjoy.

Amount per serving (4 total)

Timing Information:

Preparation	Cooking	Total Time
20 m	10 m	30 m

Nutritional Information:

Calories	399 kcal
Fat	11.3 g
Carbohydrates	60.4g
Protein	12.9 g
Cholesterol	12 mg
Sodium	99 mg

* Percent Daily Values are based on a 2,000 calorie diet.

Couscous XXVIII

(Tomatoes, Mozzarella, Basil, and Mint)

Ingredients

- 4 large tomatoes
- 1 1/2 C. vegetable broth
- 1/2 C. sun-dried tomatoes, chopped
- 1 C. couscous
- 1/4 C. shredded nonfat mozzarella cheese
- 1/4 C. chopped fresh basil
- 2 tbsps minced fresh mint leaves
- 1/4 tsp ground black pepper

Directions

- Set your oven to 375 degrees before doing anything else.

- Divide your tomatoes in two, then remove the inside flesh and place them to the side.
- Invert the skins and let them dry out on a working surface.
- While the tomatoes are drying boil the sun dried tomatoes in broth for 4 mins then pour in the couscous.
- Place a lid on the pot and shut the heat.
- Let the couscous sit for 7 mins.
- Add to your couscous: pepper, cheese, tomato insides, mint, and basil.
- Mix everything evenly. Then fill up your tomato skins with the mix.
- Put the stuffed tomatoes in a casserole dish and cook them in the oven for 32 mins.
- Enjoy.

Amount per serving (4 total)

Timing Information:

Preparation	Cooking	Total Time
25 m	30 m	55 m

Nutritional Information:

Calories	245 kcal
Fat	1.1 g
Carbohydrates	47.7g
Protein	11.4 g
Cholesterol	1 mg
Sodium	284 mg

* Percent Daily Values are based on a 2,000 calorie diet.

Couscous XXX

(Almonds, Ham, Ginger, and Broccoli)

Ingredients

- 1 1/2 C. water
- 1 C. couscous
- 2 C. chicken broth
- 1/4 C. cornstarch
- 3 tbsps soy sauce
- 3 tbsps brown sugar
- 1/8 tsp ground ginger
- 1 tbsp vegetable oil
- 2 cloves garlic, minced
- 1 (16 oz.) package mixed broccoli and cauliflower florets
- 1 carrot, sliced
- 1/4 lb cooked ham, cut into strips
- 1 (8 oz.) can sliced water chestnuts, drained
- 1/2 C. sliced almonds

Directions

- Get your couscous boiling in water for 12 mins. Then place a lid on the pot and shut the heat.
- Get a bowl, mix: ginger, broth, sugar, soy sauce, and cornstarch.
- Stir fry the following in veggie oil for 9 mins: carrots, garlic, cauliflower, and broccoli.
- Pour in the soy sauce mix and cook for 1 min. Then add the chestnuts and ham, cook for 2 more mins, while stirring, and then add in the almonds.
- Enjoy the veggies alongside or over the couscous.

Amount per serving (6 total)

Timing Information:

Preparation	Cooking	Total Time
10 m	10 m	20 m

Nutritional Information:

Calories	318 kcal
Fat	8.9 g
Carbohydrates	46.6g
Protein	12.9 g
Cholesterol	11 mg
Sodium	994 mg

* Percent Daily Values are based on a 2,000 calorie diet.

Couscous XXXI

(Feta, Cucumbers, Jalapenos, Basil, and Cilantro)

Ingredients

- 3 C. water
- 2 C. couscous
- 1/2 C. crumbled feta cheese
- 1 fresh jalapeno pepper, chopped
- 1/2 cucumber, diced
- 1 clove garlic, minced
- 1/2 C. chopped green onion
- 3 tbsps chopped fresh mint
- 3 tbsps chopped fresh basil
- 3 tbsps chopped fresh cilantro
- 1 tbsp chopped fresh parsley
- 2 tsps ground cumin
- 2 tsps cayenne pepper
- 1 lemon, juiced

Directions

- Boil your couscous in water for 2 mins, then place a lid on the pot, shut the heat, and let it sit for 7 to 10 mins.
- Once it has cooled and all the liquid has been soaked up stir the mix with a fork.
- Simultaneously add the following to a salad bowl: lemon juice, cheese, cayenne, jalapenos, cumin, cucumbers, garlic, parsley, onions, cilantro, basil, and mint.
- Mix the couscous in with other ingredients after it has finished cooking and also has cooled.
- Enjoy.

Amount per serving (6 total)

Timing Information:

Preparation	Cooking	Total Time
20 m	10 m	30 m

Nutritional Information:

Calories	210 kcal
Fat	3.3 g
Carbohydrates	38.3g
Protein	8.1 g
Cholesterol	11 mg
Sodium	155 mg

* Percent Daily Values are based on a 2,000 calorie diet.

Couscous XXXII

(Peppers, Garlic, Onions, Mushrooms, and Dates)

Ingredients

- 1 tbsp olive oil
- 1 medium onion, chopped
- 2 whole star anise pods
- salt to taste
- 3 cloves garlic, peeled and chopped
- 1/2 red bell pepper, chopped
- 2 dried hot red peppers, diced
- 1/2 tsp ground black pepper
- 4 large fresh mushrooms, chopped
- 1 tbsp lemon juice
- 1/4 C. chopped dates
- 1 tsp ground cinnamon
- 1 C. uncooked couscous
- 1 1/2 C. vegetable stock

Directions

- Stir fry your onions until soft then add in some salt and anise. Add the black pepper, garlic, hot red peppers and bell pepper too.
- Continue stir frying until these peppers become soft. Now add in the lemon juice, cinnamon, mushrooms, and dates.
- Let the date mix cook for 12 mins with a low level of heat.
- Meanwhile gently boil your couscous in the stock, in a lidded pot, for 7 mins. Then stir the couscous after it has cooled off slightly.
- Pour the stirred couscous into the date mix and stir everything.
- Enjoy.

Amount per serving (2 total)

Timing Information:

Preparation	Cooking	Total Time
10 m	20 m	30 m

Nutritional Information:

Calories	594 kcal
Fat	10.6 g
Carbohydrates	111.9g
Protein	18 g
Cholesterol	0 mg
Sodium	315 mg

* Percent Daily Values are based on a 2,000 calorie diet.

Couscous XXXIII

(Cucumbers, Capers, and Dates)

Ingredients

- 1 skinless, boneless chicken breast half
- 1/2 C. couscous
- 1/2 C. water
- 1 tbsp unsalted butter
- 1 pinch salt
- 1 tbsp salted butter
- 1/4 C. capers, drained
- 3 dates, pitted and chopped
- 1/4 C. mascarpone cheese
- 1/4 C. heavy cream
- salt and ground black pepper to taste (optional)
- 1 date, pitted and chopped
- 1/4 cucumber, diced
- 1/2 tomato, diced
- 1 tsp lemon juice (optional)

Directions

- Grill your chicken for 7 mins per side. Then divide it into two pieces.
- Boil your water with some salt and butter. Then pour in the couscous, place a lid on the pot, shut the heat to the stove, and let the contents sit for 12 mins.
- Let it cool and then stir it.
- Stir fry your dates and capers for a few mins in the butter then add in the cream and the cheese. Let the cheese mix cook for 4 mins.
- Place your couscous on serving platter add a diced date and then some cheese sauce and then the chicken.
- Add some chopped tomatoes and cucumber with some lemon juice as well.
- Enjoy.

Amount per serving (2 total)

Timing Information:

Preparation	Cooking	Total Time
30 m	25 m	55 m

Nutritional Information:

Calories	616 kcal
Fat	37.5 g
Carbohydrates	50.6g
Protein	21.9 g
Cholesterol	140 mg
Sodium	616 mg

* Percent Daily Values are based on a 2,000 calorie diet.

Couscous XXXIV

(Kebabs)

(Moroccan Style VI

Ingredients

- 1 (8 oz.) package tempeh, cut into 1/2 inch squares
- 16 fresh white mushrooms
- 1 medium eggplant, cut into 1 inch cubes
- 1 large red bell pepper, cut into 1 inch pieces
- 16 cherry tomatoes
- 8 tbsps olive oil
- 4 tbsps soy sauce
- 4 tbsps teriyaki sauce
- 3 tbsps honey
- 1 tbsp grated fresh ginger root
- 1 tbsp chopped fresh garlic
- salt and pepper to taste
- 2 C. vegetable broth
- 1 tbsp grated fresh ginger root

- 1 tsp ground cumin
- salt to taste
- 1 C. dry couscous
- 3/4 C. raisins
- 3/4 C. drained canned chick-peas (garbanzo beans)
- 1 lemon

Directions

- Get a bowl, combine the following: black pepper, tomatoes, olive oil, bell peppers, salt, soy sauce, eggplants, garlic (1 tbsp), tempeh, teriyaki sauce, ginger (1 tbsp), mushrooms, and honey.
- Place plastic wrap around the bowl and place everything in the fridge for 1 to 2 hours.
- Get the following boiling: salt, veggie stock, cumin, and ginger (1 tbsp).
- Once boiling pour in your couscous, beans, and raisins.

- Place a lid on the pot, shut the heat, and leave it for 7 mins.
- Once the couscous has cooled, add some fresh squeezed lemon juice over it.
- Stake your veggies on skewers and then grill them until the veggies are done, and have grill marks.
- Serve your kebabs with the couscous.

NOTE: If you prefer to not use a grill you can cook the kebabs under the broiler.

Amount per serving (4 total)

Timing Information:

Preparation	Cooking	Total Time
30 m	15 m	2 h 45 m

Nutritional Information:

Calories	820 kcal
Fat	35.3 g
Carbohydrates	110.1g
Protein	26.8 g
Cholesterol	0 mg
Sodium	2132 mg

* Percent Daily Values are based on a 2,000 calorie diet.

Couscous XXXV

(Carrots, Harissa, Peppers, Chicken, and Sausage)

Ingredients

- 3 tbsp olive oil
- 2 lbs chicken thighs
- 12 oz. Italian sausage
- 1 tbsp diced garlic
- 2 onions, minced
- 2 carrots, julienned
- 1/2 stalk celery, chunked
- 1 rutabaga, parsnip, or turnip, chunked
- 1/2 green bell pepper, julienned
- 1/2 red bell pepper, julienned
- 1 can diced tomatoes
- 1 can garbanzo beans
- 2 C. chicken stock
- 2 tsps thyme
- 1 tsp turmeric
- 1 tsp cayenne pepper

- 1/4 tsp harissa
- 1 bay leaf
- 2 zucchini, cut in half
- 2 C. couscous
- 2 C. chicken stock
- 1/2 C. plain yogurt

Directions

- Brown your chicken thighs all over in olive oil.
- Add in your sausage and cook everything until fully done. Once it has cooled dice the sausage into pieces.
- Now stir fry your garlic and onions until tender and see-through then combine in: stock, bay leaf, carrots, harissa, beans, celery, cayenne, tomatoes, turmeric, rutabaga, thyme, red and green peppers.
- Cook for 2 more mins before adding your chicken and sausage.

- Place a lid on the pan and cook for 35 mins until chicken is fully done.
- Add your zucchini and cook for 7 more mins.
- Meanwhile boil 2 C. of chicken stock then pour it over your couscous in a bowl along with 2 tbsps of olive oil.
- Place a covering on the bowl and let it sit for at least 10 mins.
- When plating the dish first layer couscous then some chicken mix and then some yogurt.
- Enjoy.

Amount per serving (6 total)

Timing Information:

Preparation	Cooking	Total Time
45 m	45 m	1 h 30 m

Nutritional Information:

Calories	934 kcal
Fat	39 g
Carbohydrates	80.5g
Protein	62.2 g
Cholesterol	169 mg
Sodium	601 mg

* Percent Daily Values are based on a 2,000 calorie diet.

Couscous XXXVI

(Garlic, Kale, and Parmesan)

Ingredients

- 1 C. water
- 2 tbsps butter
- 1 C. whole wheat couscous
- 2 tbsps extra-virgin olive oil
- 1 (15 oz.) can cannellini beans, drained and rinsed
- 1 C. chopped kale
- 4 cloves garlic, chopped
- 1/4 C. whole salted almonds, halved
- 1/4 C. grated Parmesan cheese
- salt and freshly ground black pepper to taste

Directions

- Boil your couscous in butter and water.
- Once boiling place a lid on the pot, shut the heat, and let it stand for 7 mins.
- Once it has cooled off stir the mix with a fork.
- Stir fry garlic, kale, and beans in olive oil for 9 mins.
- Combine the bean mix with the couscous and then add the almonds.
- Add your preferred amount of pepper and salt and then garnish your servings with parmesan.
- Enjoy.

Amount per serving (4 total)

Timing Information:

Preparation	Cooking	Total Time
15 m	5 m	25 m

Nutritional Information:

Calories	432 kcal
Fat	19.2 g
Carbohydrates	51.1g
Protein	13.9 g
Cholesterol	20 mg
Sodium	352 mg

* Percent Daily Values are based on a 2,000 calorie diet.

Couscous XXXVII

(Savory, Parsley, Lemon, and Tomatoes)

Ingredients

- 1 C. water
- 1 tsp dried savory
- 1 tsp dried parsley
- 1 pinch crushed red pepper flakes
- 1 tbsp chicken bouillon granules
- 1/2 C. pearl (Israeli) couscous
- 1 lemon, zest grated
- 1/2 C. toasted slivered almonds
- 1/2 C. chopped celery
- 1/3 C. chopped onion
- 1/2 tomato, seeded and chopped
- 1 tbsp olive oil
- salt and black pepper to taste

Directions

- Boil: bouillon, savory, pepper flakes, and parsley.
- Once boiling add in the couscous.
- Set the heat to low and let the contents gently boil for 12 mins.
- Place a lid on the pot and let everything cool and remove any extra liquid.
- Pour everything into a big bowl and add: olive oil, zest, tomatoes, salt, almonds, black pepper, onions, and celery.
- Place a wrapping of foil around the bowl and leave it in the fridge for 2 hrs before serving.
- Enjoy.

Amount per serving (3 total)

Timing Information:

Preparation	Cooking	Total Time
20 m	10 m	1 h 30 m

Nutritional Information:

Calories	266 kcal
Fat	14.3 g
Carbohydrates	27g
Protein	7.9 g
Cholesterol	< 1 mg
Sodium	401 mg

* Percent Daily Values are based on a 2,000 calorie diet.

Couscous XXXVIII

(Buttery Chives and Cheddar)

Ingredients

- 2 tsps butter
- 1 C. pearl (Israeli) couscous
- 2 C. chicken broth
- 1/2 C. heavy cream
- 1/4 C. diced pimientos
- 1 pinch cayenne pepper, or more to taste
- 3 oz. shredded sharp Cheddar cheese
- 1 tbsp chopped fresh chives
- salt and freshly ground black pepper to taste

Directions

- Toast your couscous in butter for 3 mins.

- Then add the broth and get everything boiling.
- Set the heat to its lowest level and let the couscous gently boil for 9 mins.
- Add the following to the couscous: cayenne, pimientos, and cream.
- Cook for 4 more mins, if the mix becomes too dry add more broth.
- Shut the heat and add in your cheddar and let it melt before adding in the chives and a bit more pepper and salt.
- Enjoy.

Amount per serving (4 total)

Timing Information:

Preparation	Cooking	Total Time
15 m	10 m	25 m

Nutritional Information:

Calories	358 kcal
Fat	20.6 g
Carbohydrates	31.3g
Protein	11.4 g
Cholesterol	71 mg
Sodium	740 mg

* Percent Daily Values are based on a 2,000 calorie diet.

Couscous XXXIX

(Tomatoes and Tarragon)

Ingredients

- 1 C. couscous
- 1 1/8 C. boiling chicken stock
- water to cover
- 2 tbsps butter
- 4 skinless, boneless chicken breast halves
- 2/3 C. heavy whipping cream
- 1/2 C. sweet corn
- 2 tomatoes, chopped
- 1/4 C. fresh chopped tarragon
- salt and pepper to taste
- 1/2 lemon, juiced

Directions

- Simmer for 4 mins, your couscous, in water and half of the stock.

- Shut the heat and place a lid on the pot.
- Stir fry your chicken in butter with the rest of the stock and cream until bubbly.
- Now add the tarragon, tomatoes, and corn, cook for 2 mins, before adding lemon juice, pepper and salt.
- Layer each plate with couscous and then the chicken mix.
- Enjoy.

Amount per serving (4 total)

Timing Information:

Preparation	Cooking	Total Time
10 m	30 m	40 m

Nutritional Information:

Calories	505 kcal
Fat	23.7 g
Carbohydrates	42.8g
Protein	30.8 g
Cholesterol	131 mg
Sodium	368 mg

* Percent Daily Values are based on a 2,000 calorie diet.

Couscous XL

(Pine Nuts, Currants, and Pork)

Ingredients

- 1 1/2 C. reduced-sodium chicken broth, divided
- 5 tbsps butter, divided
- 3/4 C. dry couscous
- 1 small onion, finely chopped
- 2 cloves garlic, minced
- 1/2 C. currants
- 1/2 C. pine nuts
- 1/8 tsp ground cinnamon
- salt and freshly ground black pepper
- 6 boneless pork loin chops, butterflied
- 1/2 C. orange marmalade

Directions

- Boil your couscous in butter (2 tbsps) and broth (1 1/4 C.) for 2 mins then shut the heat, add a lid to the pot, and let it sit for 12 mins. Once it has cooled, stir it.
- Now stir fry your garlic and onions in butter (3 tbsps) for 7 mins.
- Place the pan to the side and add in: salt, cinnamon, pepper, currants, couscous, and pine nuts.
- Add a bit more stock so that mix can be held together and then set your oven to 350 degrees before doing anything else.
- Fill your pork pieces with the couscous mix and stake each one with a tooth pick.
- Put everything in a casserole dish that has been coated with nonstick spray and coat them with the marmalade.
- Cook the pork in the oven for 47 mins then take out the toothpicks.
- Enjoy.

Amount per serving (6 total)

Timing Information:

Preparation	Cooking	Total Time
35 m	45 m	1 h 20 m

Nutritional Information:

Calories	500 kcal
Fat	23.1 g
Carbohydrates	46.6g
Protein	28.7 g
Cholesterol	85 mg
Sodium	151 mg

* Percent Daily Values are based on a 2,000 calorie diet.

Couscous XLI

(Bacon, Balsamic, and Curry)

Ingredients

- 4 slices bacon
- 1 onion, chopped
- 1 1/2 C. water
- 1 C. uncooked couscous
- 3/4 C. diced carrot
- 3/4 C. diced cucumber
- 1/2 red bell pepper, diced
- 1/2 (15 oz.) can garbanzo beans, drained and rinsed
- 1/4 C. olive oil
- 2 tbsps white balsamic vinegar
- 1 tbsp soy sauce
- 1 tbsp white sugar
- 2 tsps curry powder
- salt and pepper to taste

Directions

- Stir fry your bacon for 11 mins and place everything on paper towels.
- Now stir fry your onions in bacon drippings and then set it to the side.
- Boil your couscous in water. Then place a lid on it and let it sit for 7 mins before stirring it after it has cooled.
- Get a bowl, combine: beans, onions, bell peppers, carrots, and cucumbers.
- Get a 2nd bowl, combine: pepper, olive oil, salt, vinegar, curry, soy sauce, and sugar.
- Top the couscous with the dressing mix and add the bacon bits.
- Enjoy.

Amount per serving (8 total)

Timing Information:

Preparation	Cooking	Total Time
25 m	5 m	50 m

Nutritional Information:

Calories	212 kcal
Fat	9.1 g
Carbohydrates	26.6g
Protein	5.9 g
Cholesterol	5 mg
Sodium	283 mg

* Percent Daily Values are based on a 2,000 calorie diet.

Couscous XLII

(Pecans, Parmesan, and Pesto)

Ingredients

- 2/3 C. pecan pieces
- 1 tbsp butter
- 1 1/2 C. quartered fresh button mushrooms
- 1 onion, chopped
- 1 tbsp minced fresh garlic
- 2 tsps butter
- 1 1/4 C. water
- 1 (5.8 oz.) box couscous
- 1 (8.5 oz.) bottle sun-dried tomato pesto
- 1/3 C. finely grated Parmesan cheese, or more to taste
- salt and ground black pepper to taste

Directions

- Toast your pecans in the oven in a casserole dish for 25 mins.
- Meanwhile stir fry the garlic, onions, and mushrooms in 1 tbsp of butter for 9 mins. Then place it all in a bowl.
- Melt 2 more tbsp of butter and then add in your water get it boiling.
- Once everything is boiling add your couscous to a big bowl and then combine it with the boiling water.
- Place a covering on the bowl of plastic wrap and let it sit for 12 mins.
- After all the liquid has been absorbed stir it with a fork.
- Add the pesto, pecans, parmesan, and mushrooms to the couscous and then add some pepper and salt.
- Mix everything evenly.
- Enjoy.

Amount per serving (4 total)

Timing Information:

Preparation	Cooking	Total Time
20 m	30 m	50 m

Nutritional Information:

Calories	471 kcal
Fat	31.3 g
Carbohydrates	38.8g
Protein	11.3 g
Cholesterol	19 mg
Sodium	222 mg

* Percent Daily Values are based on a 2,000 calorie diet.

Couscous XLIII

(Honey Rutabaga)

Ingredients

- 1 rutabaga, chunked
- 2 C. water
- 1 tbsp vegetable oil
- 1 1/2 C. couscous
- 1/2 C. nutritional yeast
- 1/4 C. vegetable oil
- 1/4 C. apple cider vinegar
- 1 1/2 tsps honey
- 1 tsp Italian seasoning
- 1 tsp dried oregano
- 1 tsp dried dill weed
- 1/2 tsp ground black pepper
- 1/4 tsp cayenne pepper
- 1 pinch salt to taste (optional)

Directions

- Steam your rutabaga over 2 inches of boiling water for 12 mins with a steamer insert.
- Boil 1 tbsp of veggie oil with 2 C. of water then add in the couscous and shut the heat after placing a lid on the pot.
- Let this sit for 15 mins before stirring after it has cooled.
- Get a bowl, combine: cayenne, veggie oil, black pepper, vinegar, dill, honey, oregano, and Italian seasonings.
- Add the rutabaga, couscous, and some salt to the dressing mix.
- Toss the contents to coat everything evenly.
- Enjoy.

Amount per serving (6 total)

Timing Information:

Preparation	Cooking	Total Time
15 m	20 m	35 m

Nutritional Information:

Calories	330 kcal
Fat	12.3 g
Carbohydrates	44.2g
Protein	11.7 g
Cholesterol	0 mg
Sodium	89 mg

* Percent Daily Values are based on a 2,000 calorie diet.

Couscous XLIV

(Green Beans and Black Beans)

Ingredients

- 2 tsps vegetable oil
- 1 medium onion, chopped
- 2 cloves garlic, minced
- 1 1/2 lbs butternut squash, peeled and cut into bite-size pieces
- 1 (14.5 oz.) can diced tomatoes with chilies
- 1 (14.5 oz.) can vegetable broth
- 1/2 C. water
- 1 tsp ground cumin
- 1 tsp dried oregano
- 1/4 tsp black pepper
- 1 (14.5 oz.) can Green Beans, undrained
- 1 (15 oz.) can black beans, rinsed and drained
- Hot cooked couscous
- Chopped fresh cilantro (optional)

Directions

- Stir fry your garlic and onion for 7 mins in oil. Then add in: black pepper, squash, oregano, diced tomatoes, cumin, water, and broth.
- Get everything boiling for 2 mins, then lower the heat and let the veggies gently boil for 32 mins covered with a lid.
- After 32 mins add both of the beans and cook for 7 more mins.
- Add some cilantro as a garnish.
- Enjoy.

Amount per serving (6 total)

Timing Information:

Preparation	Cooking	Total Time
25 m	35 m	1 h

Nutritional Information:

Calories	262 kcal
Fat	2.2 g
Carbohydrates	52.2g
Protein	10.2 g
Cholesterol	0 mg
Sodium	843 mg

* Percent Daily Values are based on a 2,000 calorie diet.

Couscous XLV

(Tabbouleh I)

Ingredients

- 1 C. low-sodium chicken broth
- 1/2 C. water
- 1 C. couscous
- 1 cucumber, seeded and diced
- 3 green onions, chopped
- 1 carrot, grated
- 1 C. chopped fresh parsley
- 1/4 C. extra-virgin olive oil
- 1/4 C. lemon juice
- 1/4 tsp ground cumin
- 1/2 tsp salt
- 1/2 tsp ground black pepper
- 1/4 C. crumbled feta cheese

Directions

- Boil your couscous in broth and water then place a lid on the pan

and shut the heat. Let the contents sit for 12 mins then stir it.
- Get a big bowl, combine: parsley, couscous, carrots, onions, and cucumbers with lemon juice and olive oil.
- Add in some black pepper, cumin, and salt before adding in the cheese.
- Enjoy.

Amount per serving (4 total)

Timing Information:

Preparation	Cooking	Total Time
25 m	5 m	35 m

Nutritional Information:

Calories	309 kcal
Fat	16.6 g
Carbohydrates	33.3g
Protein	7.6 g
Cholesterol	9 mg
Sodium	454 mg

* Percent Daily Values are based on a 2,000 calorie diet.

Couscous XLVI

(Scallops, Parsley, and Parmesan)

Ingredients

- 2 1/2 C. water
- 2 tbsps butter, divided
- 1 tsp salt
- 2 C. pearl (Israeli) couscous
- 1/4 C. extra-virgin olive oil
- 1/4 C. white wine
- 2 tsps grated Parmesan cheese
- 3 cloves garlic, minced
- 1/4 C. chopped fresh parsley
- salt and ground black pepper to taste
- 1 lb bay scallops
- 4 tsps grated Parmesan cheese, or to taste - divided (optional)
- 1 tbsp chopped fresh parsley, or to taste (optional)

Directions

- Boil a tbsp of butter, and salt in water then pour in the couscous and lower the heat.
- Let the couscous gently boil for 12 mins uncovered.
- Stir fry the following spices in butter (1 tbsp) and olive oil for 6 mins to season the butter: parsley, pepper, salt, wine, garlic, parmesan.
- Turn up the heat and add in your scallops and cook for 5 more mins.
- Plate your couscous then add a topping of scallops and also some more parmesan.
- Enjoy.

Amount per serving (4 total)

Timing Information:

Preparation	Cooking	Total Time
15 m	20 m	35 m

Nutritional Information:

Calories	566 kcal
Fat	22.1 g
Carbohydrates	50.4g
Protein	37.1 g
Cholesterol	87 mg
Sodium	1015 mg

* Percent Daily Values are based on a 2,000 calorie diet.

Couscous XLVII

(Lentils, Onions, Feta, and Cranberries)

Ingredients

- 1 C. dried lentils
- 2 bay leaves, divided (optional)
- water to cover
- 2 C. water
- 1 C. couscous

Dressing:
- 3 tbsps lemon juice
- 1 tsp honey
- 1 tbsp white wine vinegar
- 1/4 tsp salt
- 3 tbsps olive oil
- ground black pepper to taste
- 1/2 C. coarsely chopped walnuts, toasted
- 1/2 C. dried cranberries, or to taste
- 1/2 C. crumbled feta cheese

- 1 small green onion, finely chopped

Directions

- Boil your lentils and bay leaf for 32 mins with a low level of heat. Remove any excess liquid.
- Boil your couscous in water, then shut the heat, place a lid on the pot.
- Let the contents sit for 7 mins before stirring it.
- Combine the couscous and lentils.
- Get a bowl, combine: lemon juice, honey, salt, green onions, walnuts, cheese, and cranberries, olive oil, vinegar, and black pepper.
- Top the couscous mix with the lemon juice mix.
- Place everything in the fridge for 30 mins to chill then serve.
- Enjoy.

Amount per serving (12 total)

Timing Information:

Preparation	Cooking	Total Time
15 m	45 m	2 h

Nutritional Information:

Calories	205 kcal
Fat	8.9 g
Carbohydrates	24.7g
Protein	7.8 g
Cholesterol	6 mg
Sodium	123 mg

* Percent Daily Values are based on a 2,000 calorie diet.

Couscous XLVIII
(Pine Nuts and Oranges)

Ingredients

- 1 (10 oz.) box uncooked plain couscous
- 1 (11 oz.) can mandarin oranges, drained and liquid reserved
- 1/4 C. pine nuts, lightly toasted

Directions

- Boil your couscous in the mandarin liquid.
- Then shut the heat, place a lid on the pot, and let the couscous sit for 10 mins until all the liquid has been absorbed, then stir.
- Add in your pine nuts and oranges.
- Enjoy.

Amount per serving (4 total)

Timing Information:

Preparation	Cooking	Total Time
5 m	15 m	20 m

Nutritional Information:

Calories	344 kcal
Fat	4.8 g
Carbohydrates	63.6g
Protein	11.6 g
Cholesterol	0 mg
Sodium	11 mg

* Percent Daily Values are based on a 2,000 calorie diet.

Couscous XLIX

(Buttery Rosemary)

Ingredients

- 1 C. water
- 1/3 C. white cooking wine
- 1 tbsp butter
- 1/2 tsp dried rosemary, crushed
- 1/4 tsp salt
- 1 C. couscous, regular or whole wheat

Directions

- Boil everything except the couscous for 2 mins then pour in the couscous, place a lid on the pot, and let the contents sit for 7 mins with no heat.
- Fluff the couscous with a fork after all the liquid has been absorbed.

- Enjoy.

Amount per serving (4 total)

Timing Information:

Preparation	Cooking	Total Time
15 m		15 m

Nutritional Information:

Calories	202 kcal
Fat	3.2 g
Carbohydrates	33.6g
Protein	5.6 g
Cholesterol	8 mg
Sodium	299 mg

* Percent Daily Values are based on a 2,000 calorie diet.

Couscous L

(Mexican Pineapple and Beans)

Ingredients

- 1/2 C. water
- 1 (15 oz.) can pineapple chunks, drained (juice reserved)
- 1 C. couscous
- 1 (15 oz.) can black beans, rinsed and drained
- 1/3 C. warm water
- 2 tbsps taco seasoning mix

Directions

- Boil .5 C. of water along with the pineapple juice then add in your couscous and place a lid on the pot after shutting the heat.
- Let the couscous sit for 7 mins before stirring it.

- Stir fry the beans and pineapple with taco seasoning and 1/3 C. of water for 8 mins.
- Then top your couscous with the pineapple mix.
- Enjoy.

Amount per serving (2 total)

Timing Information:

Preparation	Cooking	Total Time
10 m	10 m	25 m

Nutritional Information:

Calories	675 kcal
Fat	1.3 g
Carbohydrates	141.2g
Protein	24.7 g
Cholesterol	0 mg
Sodium	1486 mg

* Percent Daily Values are based on a 2,000 calorie diet.

Couscous LI

(Crab, Clams, Bok Choy, and Tomatoes)

Ingredients

- 2 tbsps butter
- 3 tbsps minced garlic
- 2 heads bok choy, chopped
- 1 (15 oz.) can corn, undrained
- 2 (10 oz.) cans baby clams, undrained
- 1 (8 oz.) bottle clam juice
- 1 (14.5 oz.) can diced tomatoes
- 2 C. water
- 1 cube vegetable bouillon
- 1 1/2 C. couscous
- 1 (4.25 oz.) can crabmeat
- 1 C. heavy cream
- 1/4 C. lime juice
- 1 C. red wine
- 2 tsps garlic salt
- 1 tsp ground black pepper

Directions

- Stir fry your bok choy and garlic in butter for 7 mins then add in: couscous, corn, bouillon, clams and juice, water, and tomatoes.
- Set your heat to low and then add in: black pepper, crabmeat, garlic salt, cream, red wine, and lime juice.
- Cook everything for 32 mins uncovered with low heat.
- Enjoy hot.

Amount per serving (6 total)

Timing Information:

Preparation	Cooking	Total Time
15 m	40 m	55 m

Nutritional Information:

Calories	626 kcal
Fat	21.9 g
Carbohydrates	61.8g
Protein	39.5 g
Cholesterol	145 mg
Sodium	1292 mg

* Percent Daily Values are based on a 2,000 calorie diet.

Couscous LII

(Saffron and Harissa)

(Persian Style)

Ingredients

- 2 tbsps warm water
- 5 saffron threads, or more to taste
- 1 C. couscous
- 1 C. vegetable broth
- 1 celery stalk, diced
- 1/4 C. dried currants
- 2 tbsps extra-virgin olive oil
- 1 tbsp lemon juice
- 1 tsp harissa, or to taste
- 1/2 tsp ground cumin
- sea salt to taste

Directions

- Get a bowl, mix: saffron and warm water.

- Boil your couscous in broth then shut the heat after placing a lid on the pot.
- Let the contents stand for 7 mins before stirring the couscous.
- Get a bowl, combine: sea salt, saffron mix, cumin, couscous, celery, harissa, currants, lemon juice, olive oil.
- Place everything in the fridge for 35 mins.
- Enjoy.

Amount per serving (4 total)

Timing Information:

Preparation	Cooking	Total Time
15 m		50 m

Nutritional Information:

Calories	265 kcal
Fat	7.3 g
Carbohydrates	43.2g
Protein	6.3 g
Cholesterol	0 mg
Sodium	228 mg

* Percent Daily Values are based on a 2,000 calorie diet.

THANKS FOR READING! NOW LET'S TRY SOME SUSHI....

Send the Book!

To grab this book simply follow the link mentioned above, or tap the book cover.

This will take you to a page where you can simply enter your email address and a PDF version of the book will be emailed to you.

I hope you are ready for some serious Sushi!

Send the Book!

You will also receive updates about all my new books when they are free.

Also don't forget to like and subscribe on the social networks. I love meeting my readers. Links to all my profiles are below so please click and connect :)

Facebook

Twitter

Come On...
Let's Be Friends :)

I adore my readers and love connecting with them socially. Please follow the links below so we can connect on Facebook, Twitter, and Google+.

Facebook

Twitter

I also have a blog that I regularly update for my readers so check it out below.

My Blog

Can I Ask A Favour?

If you found this book interesting, or have otherwise found any benefit in it. Then may I ask that you post a review of it on Amazon? Nothing excites me more than new reviews, especially reviews which suggest new topics for writing. I do read all reviews and I always factor feedback into my newer works.

So if you are willing to take ten minutes to write what you sincerely thought about this book then please visit our Amazon page and post your opinions.

Again thank you!

INTERESTED IN OTHER EASY COOKBOOKS?

Everything is easy! Check out my Amazon Author page for more great cookbooks:

For a complete listing of all my books please see my author page.

Printed in Great Britain
by Amazon